JOURNEYS

POEMS

BY

Janette B. Pratt

susannasheehy@yahoo.com

ISBN 978-0-9836471-0-2

Elden Publishing, LLC

For what is a poem but a hazardous attempt
at self-understanding:
it is the deepest part of autobiography.

Robert Penn Warren

MORNING IN A LANCASHIRE MILL TOWN

I wake in morning dark to the sound of the factory whistle

Warm in my bed, I see my breath in icy air as I listen

Outside the window, clogs clatter on the cobblestones,

Workers chatter, voices raised in cheerful greeting.

Time ticks away and now

Clattering becomes faster, running, voices urgent

Do not be late! Do not be late!

The second whistle sounds and, reluctant, I rise

Shivering into my cold clothes, I go to school.

Every Street

The houses line the narrow pavement,
Stretching in long unbroken row between
the corner shop and the pub
Each sharing its walls with its neighbors.
Erected years before those who must live there
could dream of a sliver of garden green
Passersby might perch upon a
windowsill, to rest or strike a match
and perhaps snatch a glance through the
chinks of ill-drawn curtains.

Come daylight, doors open and those in work come first
hurrying to beat the relentless factory clock.
School children next – giggling girls with swinging book bags
Pretending not to see the jostling boys who grab a cap
from the smallest and tossing it, laugh as he struggles to retrieve it.
Now women with babies in prams or wailing toddlers
fresh from their beds and thrust into battered strollers
string bags hanging from the handles.
Last, the old or idle who loiter exchanging gossip
as they wait upon the opening of the pub.

As the daylight dies, the hours bring
them home for tea and doors open and close again.
Televisions flicker on, children worry over homework,
kettles whistle and women warm plates over the stove
as they peel potatoes and eke out another sliver of meat
 from an already well eaten chicken carcass.
Then there is the pub or the bed
As the street settles into its nightly slumber
And houses await the next dawn.

AN ORDINARY LIFE

Born when the aging Queen dallied on the hearth
with her Scottish groom
Under skies coal -darkened by the smoke from mill chimneys,
Her father, shabby, clump booted crossed the fields to pile stones
 Making walls to fence the sheep
At night she was sent to the pub to bring him home
before the hard-earned wage was all spent.

At school, boys kicked each other laughing
Before. still children, they vanished into mills or mines.
She, young teen too went to work at the mill,
amid the clattering of the looms in the weaving shed
Where growing older, she found a man to share the life she had.
Though any dreamt of future vanished early.

Afterwards lean years became still leaner
Looms fell silent and hungry workers crowded street corners,
Only the pub she had long hated seemingly still alive.
Till another conflict took the men away and brought
a rain of devastation
 lighting the night sky with fire as it swept away homes and lives.
 And word of soldiers lost again, in Europe again,
the place, she thought, wars always began.

She saw the arrival of the car, the radio,
telephone and television and other
Inventions she neither imagined nor wanted.
Airplanes too though she never flew in one, nor considered it
She saw people turn away from chapel
and think they turned only to pleasure
Her birth Queen long gone, she watched that monarch's
 great-great granddaughter take her turn upon the throne.
And there upon the TV screen flickering in white and grey
A man walked on the moon.

Living to see her world lost and a new one,
Not changed for the better in her eyes.
No-one left alive to share her memories
Not famous or rich or revered
Holding tight to her principles
Lamenting change, holding on to the end
Of just an ordinary life.

ILFRACOMBE*

Albert was a hard man, dour
Short of speech and shorter yet of smile or laugh,
His wife, poor Edith, half-crippled, limping, no longer
Hopeful of joy or even kindness
Talked wistfully of that magical place
Of Ilfracombe.
I still remember the smell of boiled cabbage
And old woolens,
The shabby gloom of the dusty, dim room.
She talked of eating ices as they walked
Arm in arm along the promenade in the sunshine,
Steps springful with youth, hearts filled with romance.
Albert, hunched silent before the flickering black and white
Of his ancient television set
Cast her a glare of disgust and snarled "Give Over"
And Ilfracombe died away.
Edith fed me strawberries for Sunday tea
And lit her grey world a little with the
Memory of that place
Of Ilfracombe.

*Ilfracombe is a seaside resort on the north Devon coast.

WE WERE LABOUR

We were Labour when it meant something
Before it was led by those Pouncey men
With their public-school ties and BBC voices
When Labour meant working men
Gathering from the mine or mill
At the Labour Club,
Wearing the red rosette and singing
"The Workers' Flag"-first verse only.

Not revolutionaries with desire to overthrow
For we were still monarchists for the most part
Respectful of George and his daughter too
Though not so much the younger lot
Who were too much in the Sunday press.
Just men and women proud to work
With their hands to put food on the table
And shoes on the feet of their children

Supporting our footballers, enjoying a pint,
Lifting our voices in glorious choirs
Not complaining -except at home
Shopping thriftily at market stalls
Lucky to spend wakes week in a boarding house
On the North Wales coast in July
Keeping firm our traditions
We were Labour!

THE HOUSE PAINTER

Noses may wrinkle at the acrid smell
Of drying paint
But for me, it is the smell of a small girl's
Happiness.
For the smell brings memories
Of early childhood
Gathering for the twelve 'o clock meal
We called "dinner"
While father washed his hands
And mother bustled to get the hot plate
To the table at the precise moment he sat.
For the smell of paint brought
Not cheer for he was seldom a cheerful man
But a certain ease on which I could rely
The smell of paint meant he was in work.

FRIENDS

Remember In youth, we danced and shared
Our confidences in the dark.
We sat at rows of desks, teachers droning
We talked of boys, disgusting and
Those perhaps less so.

Now seen less often than before
Across space, raising children
Negotiating marriage
Meeting not often but always
with pleasure.

Older now and aware of our creaking health
We try to find our way
In our world changed by time and loss
Hoping for a moment when we might meet again
To share memories
To be as we ever were, friends.

PLATFORM 2

She waits for the train, umbrella in hand
It had rained earlier,
Take your brolly
Her mother said
And she always did
 as her mother said
But not for long she thought watching
The empty train lines
Birds perched on the wires above
And beyond the blind eyes of houses
Laundry on the line,
How do they bear the noise she thought?
The train came around the bend
Rattling and brakes squeaking
Came suddenly to a halt
She stepped aboard, stowing her suitcase
Folding the umbrella
Straightening her skirt, the red corduroy skirt
Of the suit her mother made.
Sitting back to the engine so she could see
The last sight of the past as it rocketed away,
In her hand was her ticket.
Her ticket to imagined adventure
At last!

THE TONTINE

A group of students gathered.
Shared experience
Only of the lecture
In rules of survivorship
Described by the professor that day
To commit them to memory
They made a tontine.

Clever minds idly over beer
Making the rules,
Solemn promises exchanged
The last one standing
Would win
And claim the prize
The tontine prize

What was the prize you ask?
Could it have been money?
No- for some us had none to give
Others too kind to say they knew
Perhaps a picture, a photo
Of us then? No? A book?
What was the tontine prize?

And who might collect?

The group is gone, dead or far scattered

And who would remember the rules?

Who remembers the prize?

For in the end it was not the prize

We wished to remember

It was the tontine.

LETTERS

Letters have been found scratched
On tree bark from Roman soldiers
Begging for more cloaks or sandals
Against the northern weather
Wishing good health to the reader
As they make their requests
To better encourage fulfillment.

Letters too from the camps of a thousand wars
From soldiers who have survived the horrors of the day
And must rise the next to face the enemy again
Or from the lower decks of pitching ships
From field hospitals where the news is uncertain
And likely to be bad
Greetings not shared face to face.

Now I have a letter and I turn it in my hands
I try to guess the contents but to hear of illness
Or worse dying would be outside my expectations
Not a bill: they have an unmistakable look
Like missives from the government – no mystery there.
Nor another urgent request to donate to
The worthy causes I would support if I could

No a personal letter: now so rare and so welcomed.

No longer begging for help scratched on tree bark

Or scrawled by candlelight in times of struggle

Just words of thanks, of cheers, of sympathy

From miles away or from a neighbor

Notes that make us smile.

A good letter.

THE GIFT

It is a book, an old book now with musty pages
Given long ago when the man is young
Given as a first token, not too costly
Not presuming, well suited to its moment.

And it is accepted gracefully the woman recalls
Liking the young man and wondering if
This token may be a first step to something
Other. More intimate.

And so it proves as the two decide
To share their lives for a time
Until by tragic chance they are parted
No longer walking a together life

And the book is put away, stored
Fading unseen and unread
Growing old too in the waiting
Till that young old woman finds it again.

IS IT RAINING?

I look up: only blue sky
No clouds in sight, just sun
A beautiful sunny day
But my face is wet
My hands too,
But why I puzzle
Am I crying?

I have had loss- who has not?
It is to be borne.
And felt guilt too
For the little unkindness's
For the sarcastic word
Now beyond retraction
But surely, I am not crying!

To cry would be selfish
To put my loss forward
Put it before others
I must not make a scene
I look again at the sky, peering
There I see it. A tiny cloud!
I knew it! Knew it must be raining!

WINTER TREE

Tall, outside my window, grey gaunt against the winter sky
It stretches bare branches towards me,
Probing, inquiring, asking, seeking comfort in its cold loneliness.
But I know soon enough it will bud with spring green
And blue-purple wisteria will climb up its trunk,
then it will turn away, like a grown child in its satisfaction
Seeking not me but the bright sun of the wider world.
But it will return, the prodigal, in the winter,
Probing, inquiring, asking, seeking again.
Shall I be here?

DEATH OF A CEDAR WAX-WING

On a frosty morning, dead upon the iron table,
glossy brown feathers, yellow breast, beak and toes upturned,
The bright-eyed squirrel on the balcony rail
scampers away not answering my unspoken question.
How did you die? Where is your family? Your friends?
Are you alone you most social of birds?
I shade my eyes to look to the far treetops
And there they are – brothers, sisters, children, friends all
upon the branches, clustered, whispering amongst themselves,
And as I watch, they turn as one and, in a flock rise into the sky.
Their comrade is gone, forgotten, the frozen body left to me.

ATTACK

The robin throws himself angrily against the window
And cannot be deterred.
For in that window, he sees another robin
Bigger perhaps and perilously near
The branch on which a nest is built and his mate
Sits on her clutch of eggs.
Every day he returns to fight that bird
Rearing up wings spread, beak pecking at the glass.
If enemy there is, he will defend.
As fierce as any father with threatened young.
What an example he is to the careless world,
He knows his parental duty and will fulfill it
Until the babies fledge and his mission is fulfilled
And he can forget that wretched imaginary enemy!
At least until next year!

THE TORTOISE

At a year, it can be held in the palm
Small and hard with scrabbling legs,
Ten years slowly growing until it is heavy in that hand
Twenty years, the palm is older now, but the tortoise still young.
How many years will it be before it is the age to remember?
To seek its fortune beyond the inches of ground slowly covered.
How many more years before it reaches full size and is comfortable
in its own shell?
It will see children born and grow old, governments formed and fall
Riches spent wisely or squandered
And it will keep its counsel on its small patch of grass
Husbanding the energy that keeps its life, however constrained.
Is this the wisest of the creatures?
Always slow to explore, expecting no surprise, wanting nothing
beyond its small world?
Is it happy with the bargain struck?
Long life but lived within a world so small?
I wonder as I watch the tortoise slowly move across the lawn
Lurching gait, head up as it seeks that fresh new green leaf.
Is it pleased with its choice or even aware of a choice made?
I wonder.

IF I WERE A BIRD

If I were to be a bird, I would wish to be an owl,
Keen-eyed, keen-eared and reputed to be wise.
Every day studying on my philosophy
On a high leafy branch or perhaps in a dark corner
Of a barn or stable.
Come twilight, I would rouse and stretch my well-rested wings
Then swoop out to find that favorite hunting spot.
Watching and listening for the incautious mouse
I sense it below rustling the leaves as it hurries home.
And in a second, I am down and it is in my sharp talons
Transformed.
If I had young ones at home, I would carry my prize to them
But most often I would satisfy my own hunger.
Perhaps then I would watch late into the night deep in thought
Until I would leisurely return home
My role well played

AT A CLINIC IN THAILAND

Brown hand dirt grained
Washed but still smelling of the soil
Wearing a clean shirt
For this occasion
In a place without running water
Or modern detergents
It is no small thing.
The arm does not lie flat
Bone once broken but not doctor set.
There is a goiter on the neck
He is not here for that
He knows there is nothing to be done.
Perhaps he has a cough
From the chemicals sprayed on fruit trees
Where he works, unprotected.
Or maybe it is his aching back
From day to night labor
Or a problem brought on by eating raw pork
Making the translator frown
Of these things he complains
With some hope of help
From within our bag of pills.
We do not share a language, a religion
Or any common experience

Except that of being human.
There we stand equal
He knows this too so
He smiles as I ask respectfully
"What is your name?"

AT THE FOOT OF THE MIHINTALE STAIRS IN SRI LANKA

Lined up there, Sri Lankan sailors
Identical in blue
With "training" stamped upon the back
Like the coat worn by a young dog as it
learns to be of service.
Why are they here,
So far from the sea or river or hint of water
At the foot of the stairs that lead
dauntingly to the sacred shrine far above?
Did they come to seek sea blessings from
A fierce land-moored god?
Ask that their ship not sink - that the hazards of their lives
be few.
If climbing long steps to reach a high shrine will do it,
Why not?

THE VILLAGE OF PENNE IN THE MASSIF CENTRAL.

The small white houses march up the hill
Flanking a steep winding road
Here a break for the well stuffed church yard
And the old church beyond it and on ridge top
The skeleton of a ruined castle against the sky.
This we can see across the valley
As on the opposite side, we settle on benches
In falling darkness and growing cold.

One by one the houses obediently
Blind the lights from their windows
Sending the village into medieval dark
The only remaining light the headlights
Of a van churning slowly up the road
Until it disappears at last over the crest of the hill.
In the darkness we wait and shiver
The Son et Lumiere is about to begin

A search light begins to pass over the dark village
Picking out an old house or two
The church and at last the castle so that each
Is illuminated in turn,
And the voice over in sonorous French
Tells us the history of this old village
I catch a few words "La Guerre Religieux"
La Plague – this is repeated often

.

Until I stop trying to understand and
Concentrate upon the moving search light
And think of other Son et Lumiere shows
I have enjoyed in warmer places
Until at last the voice dies away
We turn away stretching stiff legs
And the villagers released from their darkness
Begin again to dot the hillside with bright points of light.

CHRISTIAN RETREAT CENTER ON IONA

THE ABBEY ON IONA

Cold stone, storm-hardened against the wind,
Hard pews worn dull
Dying sunlight spilt through narrow windows
Impatiently we wait in silence
For the long whispered spirit moving in this place
That it may lift us and carry us home.

THE OTTERS' LAMENT*

Running down the stone steps
Through the echoing cloisters
Like Benedictines long ago.
Not Nones, Matins or Lauds,
But Morning Service
Calls us from the kitchen
To sing, to listen, to pray
To husband the tiny silences
And hold them briefly close
Before running back to duties left unfinished

*guests at the Abbey are divided into four service groups. The
otters are one of those groups.

AT HADRIAN'S WALL

Crossing the heath, feet high and mossy grass topped
To modern eyes, not considered much a barrier
But to those soldiers so far from home
In a world lit only by fire
And armed only with spears and discipline
It was their shelter in this cold unfamiliar country.

They had no horses to ride the moors
No cannon to fill with shot as they watched
Braving the blustery wind and sheets of rain
Huddled in their cloaks, only sandals on their feet
Peering through the distance to spy
The barbarians approaching

Quiet now, we stroll along side this inadequate wall
We remark it does not even follow modern boundaries
We see no enemy, only sheep and a well -trained dog
And we stop to watch him working as his master
Crests the hill on his tractor whistling.
And leaves him to work unaided.

Where are the barbarians now?
Or those watching soldiers who lived and died
So far from the warm sun of their homeland.
How would they recognize those barbarians now?
Enemies we fear that likely would not be
Deterred by a mossy -grass topped wall of stone.

JOURNEY FROM THE KENYAN VILLAGE

Bouncing away through the darkness
On the deeply rutted roads
A child leans across my lap
As we search the night sky
For familiar stars.
Behind us in the night babble
Of the Pokot village
Ragged children pop the last of the balloons
And peel our stickers from dusty arms
As they wait with hungry eyes
To eat the leftovers from the mzungu* feast.

*mzungu is the Swahili word for "white person"

THE EQUATOR

We all stand at the Equator
Sometimes north, sometimes south
Stepping across the invisible line.
We wonder with delight
As water seeps away
With the clock tick or against
And wonder too how far the pregnant
Woman bending over her bucket
Must travel to deliver her baby,
And if it will be safe
In the north or in the south?

MAASAI VILLAGE

She built the house dark and strong
Thick walls making small unlit spaces.
Tonight as she bends over the open fire
Smoke fills the house and the baby coughs
The baby goats stir uneasy in their crib.
She lifts her head pausing to listen, spoon in hand.
Outside is danger but she hears only the wind.
She bends over the rice pot again
Safe
In her house.

*Maasai women build their own houses in the villages for their families and livestock. Because they cook on open fires inside without ventilation, respiratory illness is common and infant mortality is high.

SINGING AT THE HOME FOR DISABLED CHILDREN IN NAROBI

Lined up in their wheelchairs, the children are frozen
Victims of disastrous births, limbs stiffened.
The wheel of life does not spin but creaks forward
To allow them to breathe and stare at us open-eyed.
What an odd group we are – the silver haired
And vigorous youth,
United in our strange whiteness.
Uneasy under their fixed gaze.

Then we sing
Those still faces slacken and gape then struggle
Into smiles
They are smiling at us! Laughing at us!
At our mangling of their language
At our awkward half-learned dance moves,
We are amusing them
Those so cursed by the life they have barely joined
And so we smile back and sing our song again.
All of us happy in the moment.

I LIKE OLD CHURCHES

I like old English churches
I like the cold stone walls
The lingering musty smell
The knobby pew ends
Set in steady rows down the aisle
Sometimes with doors
That restless children
And adults too
Like to swing and bang
Quite satisfactorily
At the more somnambulant
Moments in the service

I like the choir stalls
No room for sleeping here
Seats tilting singers forward
So they are always ready
To rise in a flock with
Music in hand
Eyes on the conductor

And behind his screen
The organist who seizes
His moment to perform
And to send resounding chords
Over those sleepy pews.
A reminder to rise and pick up the
Worn hymn book from the rack
And hope to know the tune.

I like the memorials on the walls
 Plaques of bronze or white marble
Carved with the names of the long dead
From families once stout supporters
Of this old church but now fallen away
Like those whose names are etched on

The World War I monument.
Every old church has one or many.
Sometimes with ragged flags or rosettes
Most often just names that the grieving
Are not allowed to forget for they are
Read upon the wall every Sunday morning

There will be a rood, perhaps a beautifully
Carved screen in older churches in tiny villages
That did not come to the notice of the king
In his predation or the self-=righteous
Puritans a couple of centuries after.
And if they are fortunate, a stain glass window
Held in place by well weathered lead
An altar and pulpit of course
And likely a font often discreetly at the back
As if either the baptism or the parents
Are not completely sanctioned.
Visitors are often asked to sign a book or
Perhaps buy a card or some local jam
Before leaving through surrounding gravestones
Following generations of parishioners hurrying
to beat the Godless to the pub next door.

I like old English churches.

PACKING

Make a list
That is what mother
Always said.
She did not say
Do not take more
Than you are willing
To carry.
That was me.
Lesson learned
And repeated often
Watching others
Burdened with bags
Containing what?
Clothes for every season
Is it important to be
Remembered for your clothes?
Or for your jewels you guard.
I knew someone once
Who carried stones.
Just ordinary stones.
The world has plenty of
Stones, I think.

I see no special magic in home stones.
So bring only what you could lose
Should something be mislaid
And lose no sleep over it.
And always leave room
For something you might pick up
To recall a place or people
A memory of some experience
Because that is the reason
You travel.

DUBROVNIK, CROATIA

Proud city between ancient walls
Teems now with life.
The guide sparkles with pride
As she points to the house of her birth,
Her church, her street.
Tourists stare at the grand buildings
And nod to encourage her.
But now she frowns with remembered pain
When she speaks of the siege, the hunger
The fear as bombs began to fall.
Ugly painful memories.
Beauty and tragedy in an old city
A hardened spot in a young woman's soul.

SARAJEVO ROSES

They bloom on street corners
Before churches, parks and schools.
They are under the feet of workers
Hurrying to catch their buses
And worshipers on the way to Sunday mass.
They gleam silently, the red splatters
Reflecting sunny summer days
Or wearing winter white.
Each bloom where a life was taken.
Perhaps a mother desperately seeking
Milk for her starving children,
A child sent out to gather the last
Scraps of wood to burn against the deep cold,
An old man shuffling and unsteady in his hunger.
A crack of rifle fire from the hidden sniper
And the rose blooms.
Lest the people of Sarajevo forget the four years
Of cruel siege, captured in their suffering city,
They may look down at the roses and remember.

VISITING A TEMPLE IN MYANMAR

They hurry past us
Bare feet with toughened soles
Slapping on the hard -cool marble.
Skirted men and women carry flowers
To lay before
The Great Buddha.
He sits silent,
Satisfied in gold, his hands folded
In a gesture understood by the petitioners.

We approach more slowly
Aliens to his message.
Tolerant, patient,
He knows we have no offerings
No petitions to make
Have you ever seen an angry Buddha?
He has fierce guardians but the Buddha?
No never, as he smiles
That quiet knowing Buddha smile

MORE TESTS

She does not wear a white coat
In the white coated world.
Assistants hover with clip boards,
Anxious patients search their faces
For clues.... For anything.

Now she comes to me, ice cold
Her touch is hard, her face unreadable
What do her fingers tell her?
Do I want to know?
She speaks to the air over my head
Do not like it, do not want to let it go,
Must test some more.
Below her hand, I start to protest but she shrugs
Might be nothing but if it is...something
And my heart sinks
Apologies.
I gather my patience to stand in line
With others clutching their news close
Worrying
Scheduling more tests.

REMEMBER THE MUSIC - DEMENTIA (1)

There is music in the fingers
And deep within the mind.
Even as new memories are no longer made
The mind searches in the drawers of the past.
Open one and see them.
Bach, Chopin, Beethoven, Mozart,
Filing by hopeful they will be recalled
To translate to present reality.
To summon them from the dimness
To be remembered and heard again

WALKING IN THE WOODLANDS- DEMENTIA (2)

The uneven path takes us into the trees
 As we leave the busy road behind
 The twittering song of birds
The crunch of twigs beneath our feet
Compete with the roar of traffic noise.

Deeper we go under the tall canopy
The dappled sunlight on the path ahead
Talking of Africa, of things he remembers
Things told me many times before
As if it was the first time.

He skips ahead like a child
Wobbling atop a fallen log
Stepping aside to look closer at a flower.
Looking back, I see the moment of confusion
As he wonders where he is,

In the wood's heart, we sit together on a bench
It is peaceful, he is glad to be there
It is not his first visit but he has no memory
My name? The place? He frowns for
there is no before, only now and that must be
enough.

WHY IS IT CALLED FOOTBALL?

They come from the dark tunnel into the bright light
Big men made bigger by bulky pads and helmets.
Surprisingly nimble as they cross the field
Followed by thinner men in black and white
The crowd alternately cheers and boos.
They will line up and piously remove helmets for the
National Anthem. Some may even sing along
The only sound we hear is the brave attempt of
Some singer outmatched by a difficult tune.
At last a whistle sounds and it begins.

Two lines of men bang into each other holding
Each other in carefully choreographed moves
In apparent effort to reach and hurt the lone man in the back
One or two run down the field, necks twisted back
As the ball, an odd oval shape, spirals overhead
They catch it or they do not as a whistle sounds.
The huge men reshuffle into their lines and a flag is thrown
Its meaning is mysterious to me, so I ask.
Illegal receiver, my companion mutters
Eh? What does that mean? He turns away

But why is it called football? I ask the air
Foot and ball connect hardly at all
And why is that ball, that strange shape?
To make it easier to hold he hisses
But if it is carried, I wonder aloud
Why... but his patience is running thin
It just is – OK? It just is!
Not the only illogical thing in the world I agree
But it still bothers me. Why on earth is it
Called FOOTBALL?

THE CHOIR

Notes dance on the lines
I read the soprano notes
The treble clef I learned long ago
EGBDF – FACE my piano teacher taught
She hit my knuckles with a sharp
Instrument she kept for that purpose
If my child's fingers did not
Reach the cords as she required
I did not learn from her
To my mother's despair
For she wanted to me to play
The piano she kept in the sitting room

But I do I remember how to read
The notes that now I see
And try to sing.
Around me are others
Some well trained in music
Others just liking to sing
I am somewhere in between
Trained and not
I listen to catch the tune
As the pianist begins
We are to sight read this piece
At least I am not alone
I hear others at my elbow
Their notes are sure and
Give me courage to join
The joy of singing
Not professionals we
But pleased to coax
The tune in harmony
 that makes us
A choir.

PLANT KILLER

My planter holds a pathetic begonia
Waiting patiently for water and sun
Knowing as I loom over it that I
Can kill anything!
Not my children thankfully
They escaped to successful adulthood
Nor the cats or dogs – well one dog
That have kept me company over the years.

But I defy any flower to enter
My orbit and live
Others have a way with plants
I look at them enviously
I am watering as are they
And yet, their plants thrive
And fill their porches or windowsills
With riotous color.

Do they talk gently to their plants?
I understand that helps
Perhaps they need music -a Bach piece
Or something more rousing?
For no matter how I kindly I beseech
My plants to grow
Their leaves grow brown, their stems bow
And the last flower petals fall away.

I see the cousins of my begonia
Blooming happily in their pot
While mine struggles to hold up
The one remaining petaled stalk
No gentle speech, no careful watering
Only the begonias own strength
Will prevent me from being
As always - the plant killer.

DEBORAH'S PLACE

Ringed by throbbing highways
Drivers stressed, heedless of all
In their haste and self-concern
There is an oasis of peace.
Here squirrels compete with chipmunks
To eat the bird seed
Till driven off away
By angry flapping wings.
Here trees send out their searching shoots
And reach to the sky with thirsty leaves
While moss turns the pathways
Glorious green.
And in this calm oasis dwells a woman
No less a part of this soft green place
Than all those other living creatures that
Call it home.
Being as one with the trees, the Queen Bee
Treasures its beauty and holds it close
This place.

SHELTERING IN PLACE

Thunder rumbles, sky darkens
Fat rain drops begin to hit the leaves
And walkers beneath hurry hastily
To their comfy shelters if they have them.

Caves have sheltered humans
Since before the time
We knew those it sheltered
were called by that or any name

Early peoples drew on cave walls
Hinting at thought and beauty
Ideas not yet able to be expressed
In language not yet invented.

Caves play a part in a version of a birth story
That followers believed important
And passed down the generations
Until someone thought to write it down.

Now many caves are places of exploration
And perhaps excitement artificially lit
Until the guide turns off his torch
And plunges all into deep blackness

They seldom shelter humans now
Preferring to leave their cold darkness
To the occasional sleeping bear
To the bats who have lived there all along.

Our caves are warmer and better appointed
With all we think we need for our lucky life
That would astonish those first peoples
Who claimed those sheltering caves as their own.

MY HAT

My hat is serviceable blue denim
Floppy brimmed and functional
Often stuffed into a bag
To be brought out in bright sunlight.
Oh how fretful it would have made
My mother – the maker of hats
Who would chide me for such an ordinary thing
As she reached to straighten the brim.
She would tie a ribbon around the crown
Perhaps with a fetching bow
And add flowers or leaves or lace
Anything to hand.
I have seen her take an ordinary beret
And turn it into an elaborate bonnet
Fit for Easter Sunday service.
Through the war, she kept her hat shop
Scrounging for materials
Riding the bus into the city to find
Warehouses ablaze and streets
Knee deep in glass from the night's bombing.
At least that is what she would tell me

As she fussed with my head gear.
She clung to her hats long after
They were not fashionable
Even for church and refused
The substitute head scarf of her compatriots
She mourned the hats' passing and if
By chance she had seen my denim chapeau
She would have gone to work
Mostly unappreciated.
For I wear the hat against the sun
It has no need of adornments
Nor her busy fingers.
Long stilled but remembered
Whenever I pick up my hat.

CAGES

I go alone from bed to kitchen
To living room or balcony
Till driven by my need to move
Alone I go out to walk.
Carrying with me the invisible
Walls of my cage
The few others walking pass me
with a wide arc
As if they see those walls around me
And would not pass through.

It is the time you might think
That provokes this distance
But I say not for we have all
Fashioned cages that we have long
Worn against strangers and their contagion
Not of disease but of poverty
Of needs that push them out
From their own cages to
Make demands upon us.

Near a store where I often shop,

A street woman

With collected shopping carts

Piled high with broken abandoned items

And plastic garbage bags filled

With what, not even she knows

Squats besides her treasured hoard

Her cage more visible than most

As I hurry quickly by, alone

To my comfortable shelter

Secure in my own invisible cage.

STATIONARY

We are a shabby silent lot waiting for the train
Not talking, waiting.
Behind us, a homeless man slumps against the wall
Both visible and invisible to us.

Wait! He is reading a book!
My attention is caught
What is he reading?
Too thin for the Bible I think, common
Reading material of train passengers
Or a novel of such richness and complexity
That he longer feels the hard floor
Of the station platform beneath him and
Is carried to a warmer kinder place?
Perhaps is it a biography dictated to a ghost writer
Of minor celebrity whose pinnacle of fame
Was reached within the pages of People magazine
Or a sports figure beloved or vilified?
Or maybe a book of self -improvement
So he might learn how to ask for a raise from the
Employer he does not have
Or to assemble the cabinets in a kitchen he
Does not own.

The train rolls in and we all step forward as doors open
Now I see the book is laid open across his face
So he does not see us moving away.
I open the pages of my own book and read.

I GOT A PLASTIC BAG

I did not mean to get it.
I always carry my bags
To the store
But somehow one slipped in
The bagger must have done it
Before I said, "no plastic"!

So now I have it, crinkled, glistening
Shall I add it to the landfill to live
A thousand ugly years?
Or will it wash out to sea into murky
Depths to strangle a sea turtle
Or prospecting sea bird?
Will it be caught by a breeze
And hang from a tree branch
A sad industrial flower?
Or shall I use it once for rubbish
And then consign it to the trash
And believe I did a good thing?
A lesser sin?

I got a plastic bag
The shame.

STUFF

The comedian George Carlin, foul-mouthed often
 But very funny had a comedy routine about stuff.
The stuff we surround ourselves with,
Visiting other homes we see others' stuff
And might compare to our own
Might even want but we return always to our own stuff.
And the home where we keep our stuff.
To the blue-white lamp shaped like a tea pot
And the coffee maker I use every day
The black faced rag dolls my mother made
Though she had never seen a black face
Except in a picture or on a movie screen.
The beautiful china an unexpected gift
 from a man I hardly knew once
The small brass Khmer Buddha bought
In a junk shop on a Cambodian street
The carved hippos my son brought from West Africa
Or a painting bought at a starving artist sale
When there was little money to decorate our walls

Or the beautiful flowers painted by a dear friend
Or Pendle Hill painted by my mother
As she sat with my father in their old car
On a sunny afternoon, drinking milky tea from a thermos
And eating meat and butter sandwiches on white bread
Or the quick cartoon of me done by an artist in
Havana as I was drinking a mojito in a bar once
Frequented by Ernest Hemingway
Or an odd book or a broach or necklace
Or just the balloon a dear friend gave me to celebrate
My birthday or a funny card
These things not valuable to others.
These things are my stuff.

SIMON OF CYRENE

He came in from the country
He was not a very good Jew
But it was Passover; it was tradition.
He despised the noisy crowds pushing on all sides
Selling dates or offering a common cup of water.
Thirsty, he accepted the cup and drank.

There was a roar: the crucified were coming
Three condemned men dragging heavy wood
People calling out, cursing, cheering, laughing even
He pushed forward a little to see
One, the last, was stumbling, half-falling
Soldiers prodding him up with their spears.

Damned Romans, how he hated them
And those Pharisees too, always interfering
In the country they left him alone.
Wait, was not this the man he heard rode into town
On a donkey amongst cheering crowds?
Surely it could not be the same and yet?

A soldier turned to the crowd searching
Was it for him? Surely not. what had he done?
It must be the date seller they wanted
But no, the butt of a spear in his chest
What did they want?
That he should carry that man's cross?

He could not believe it. Why him?
Shouldering the heavy wood, cursing
He caught sight of the man's face
Grateful, relief at even a moment's respite
They all moved on.
Slowly, painfully through the crowds

When they came to the place, he put down
The cross and turned away.
He had no reason to stay
But a man caught his arm
What is your name friend?

He did not want to say it
He looked up at the cross where the man
Was now fixed; he shivered,
There was something about him
So he gave the stranger his name
Simon. From Cyrene.

.

MARCHING IN ATLANTA

We are marching, walking rather, crowd huddled
As we cross the long bridge
Jostled together, signs held high.
Rain has left deep puddles beneath our feet
We plod forward careless of our shoes.
Black and white, women and men, children
Walking.
Some chant, some issue, their issue
But the crowd does not rise and the chanting dies.
Ahead the chanting begins again but most cannot hear it.
Do not need to hear it.
Walking.
March against a war that saps away our young strength
March against a system that keeps many in slavery,
Marchers are united in their diversity
March against those who would seek to return us
To an unobtainable past.
My past

RECOGNITION

Was it the margaritas we tasted at every bar on the River Walk?
Or the visit to the Alamo, so large in lore, so small in life
Or the mariachi mass in the bright white church?
Or maybe it was the bucket of mussels shared in Nova Scotia
Or the lobsters or endless glasses of Chardonnay.

Or perhaps it was eating oysters fresh from their beds
On the coast of Brittany
Or sailing from the Orkneys in an almost empty ferry
Or walking the parapets of the Rosslyn Chapel
Or visiting a stately home, a church, a graveyard and happily, a
pub.

Was it the visit to the site of the Battle of Verdun
With its sad rows of white stones
Or the castle with walls that gave the long view to the Rhine
Over which watchers might see the approaching invader
Or no it must be sailing back home across the Atlantic.

Maybe it was the time, when staying in a cottage
In a Welsh village of unpronounceable name
When we won the raffle to the consternation of the natives
Or perhaps sitting in the sun-dappled garden of dear friends
Drinking tea, tossing balls for their insistent dog.

Was it then when we had that shared moment?
A moment so special when we recognized,
What we guessed maybe from our first
Meeting but that we did not name until that moment
That we would always be best friends

BECOMING HOME (KEN'S POEM)

Morning sun through the leaves
Dapples the water.
The boat rocks gently
Eager fish are nibbling.
The only sound he hears is the
Cheerful hum of the cicadas
As a soft breeze ripples the surface of the lake.

High on the hillside above, she sits reading
Amid riotous color.
The pages of her book stir
Forgotten now as she closes her
Eyes to the sun on her face
And lifts her cheeks to feel the breeze.
becoming Home.
And they feel together the peace
Coming on that breeze.
A knowing, a comforting, a belonging
The peace
Of becoming home

OVER THE NICK OF PENDLE

The road was a river of moonlight over the purple moor
To steal an image from *The Highwayman* by Alfred Noyes
A poem I memorized in large part as a child.
I do not expect highwaymen or redcoats on my road
Though a tavern is always a welcome sight.
On my road there are wind-blown scraps of gorse
And an occasional boulder or piece of litter
Left by careless walkers ahead of me.
I could hope for a coven of witches
Should it be near All Hallow's Eve
So I search for their stone circles
And step aside for the few cyclists who attempt
To climb the long hill to reach this top place.
I see only a few grazing sheep marked with ink
To show they belong to the farm in the valley.
There is wind here with few trees to break it
Only the piled stone walls of an earlier age.
It is a place to walk. It is a place to see beyond
The town in the valley below and its car filled streets
The old brick chimneys of idle cotton mills
To see only the road winding over the moor.
It is a place where my past and present are found together
And where I might sometime catch a glimpse of
What lies beyond.